THE USBORNE BOOK OF
HORSES
AND PONIES

Lucy Smith

Designed by Jane Felstead
Additional designs by Beth Wood

Illustrated by Miranda Gray
Additional Illustrations by Stuart Trotter
Cover design by Tom Lalonde

Consultant: Susan McBane

Contents

Herds of horses

Many thousands of years ago, horses were wild animals. They roamed around in big groups called herds. People hunted them for meat and to make clothes out of their skins.

About 5,000 years ago, people began to tame horses. They used the quietest ones to carry things and pull carts. Then they started to ride the horses. Today, most horses are tame.

These horses are called mustangs. Horses like these still live free in North America.

Spanish explorers brought horses to North America about 400 years ago. Mustangs are related to those animals.

This is a mare, or grown-up female. There may be up to eight mares in a herd.

In the wild, horses mostly eat grass. Mustangs can survive on very little food.

All horses can run, or gallop, very fast. This is the only way they can escape from danger.

This is a stallion. It is a grown-up male. There is usually one in each herd.

2

First horses

Hyracotherium (say high-rack-oh-thear-ee-um) lived about 50 million years ago. It was about as tall as a fox.

Hyracotherium

Equus Caballus

Over millions of years, Hyracotherium changed. It became Equus Caballus (ek-wus cab-al-us), the first modern horse.

This mare is the leader of the herd. She decides where to look for fresh grass and when it is time to move on.

A mare and the stallion get together to make a foal. This is called mating.

There are often baby horses in a herd. They are called foals.

Horses and ponies feel safer in herds.

Arab horses

There are lots of different breeds, or kinds, of horses. People think Arab horses may be the oldest breed in the world. They probably come from the deserts of what is now Iran. They were first tamed by people who lived in the deserts.

Arab horses have big, dark eyes. Their necks are curved and they have long, very silky manes.

Arab relations

Because Arab horses are so beautiful and strong, they have been mated with other kinds to make new or better breeds. The horses below all look different, but each was made partly by breeding with Arab ones.

Andalusian

Welsh Mountain pony

You can recognize an Arab horse by its slightly curved face. Its nose and mouth are velvety and it has wide nostrils.

The coat of this Arab horse is grey. A horse which is any shade of white or grey is called a grey horse.

Percheron

Arab horses can be other shades too, such as brown or black.

In fact, most types of horses we know today are related to the Arab in some way.

The points of a horse

The different parts of any horse's body are called its points. Each part has a special name. Here are some of the main points of a horse.

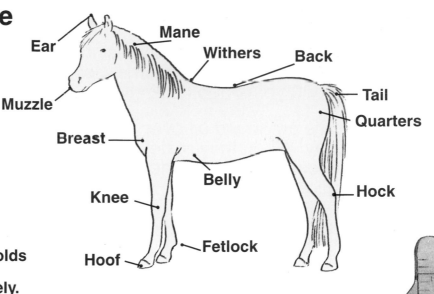

Ear
Mane
Withers
Back
Muzzle
Tail
Quarters
Breast
Belly
Hock
Knee
Fetlock
Hoof

An Arab horse holds its tail high. This makes it look lively.

Arab horses are very friendly. This may be because some desert people called the Bedouin used to keep their Arab horses with them in their tents.

Arab horses are very fast. They can keep going for a long time.

Horse or pony?

Horses and ponies are the same kinds of animals, but most horses are taller than ponies. They are all measured using a stick which has special measurements on it called hands. A hand is about 10 cm (4 inches) - about as wide as a grown-up's hand.

The height is measured from the ground to the withers. Horses are usually more than 14.3 hands high. This means fourteen hands and three inches tall. Most ponies are less than 14.3 hands.

5

Thoroughbred horses

Thoroughbreds are the fastest horses in the world. They were first used for racing about 300 years ago, in England.

Thoroughbreds are found all over the world today. When they mate with other breeds, they make them faster and more beautiful.

These Thoroughbreds are running a race called a flat race. They gallop along a track as fast as they can.

Jockeys are very light, so they do not slow their horses down.

Racing silks

When they ride in races, jockeys wear very light tops and caps called racing silks. These are bright, so people can tell the jockeys apart. Each jockey wears silks in patterns chosen by the horse's owner.

Young Thoroughbreds like these are often nervous. They can get very excited.

This dirt track is covered in wood shavings and sand. Races are also run on grass.

Jockeys lean forward and almost stand up, so they do not press on the horses' backs. This helps the horses run even faster.

Jockeys wear hard hats to stop them hurting their heads if they fall off.
In a race, they wear bright caps over the hats so people know which jockey is which.

A Thoroughbred which wins races is worth a lot of money.

This breed has long, slim legs which help it run fast.

Other kinds of horse racing

In a steeplechase, horses jump fences as they gallop along. Steeplechasers start racing when they are about five years old. They must be fully grown so that they are strong enough to jump the fences.

In a trotting race, the horses trot very fast and pull a little cart called a sulky. Most trotting horses are a breed called Standardbreds. There are lots of trotting races in France, Australia and the United States.

Foals

Foals are very playful, so it is best if they are kept with other foals as well as their mothers. They need plenty of space to leap about in so that they grow up strong and healthy.

A colt is a male foal under four years old. After that, males are called stallions.

This female foal is three months old. Until they are four years old, females are called fillies. After that, they are called mares.

These foals are playing. This helps them learn how to behave with other horses.

A foal's body grows stronger from the feet up. Its hooves and legs get harder and thicker first. Then the rest of its body grows, too.

The first few hours

Most foals are born at night, when it is dark and peaceful. The mare licks the newborn foal clean. The foal can stand after only half an hour. It starts to drink milk from its mother's udder. This is called suckling.

At first, the foal wobbles on its weak legs. After a few hours, it can walk and run.

Suckling foal

8

Most foals are born in the spring, when there is plenty of fresh, green grass for them to eat.

This foal is only a few hours old, but it is already strong enough to run next to its mother.

The foal's tail is short and fluffy. It will get longer and rougher as the foal grows up.

The foal's long legs help it keep up when its mother gallops.

Growing up

A newborn foal is about the same height as its mother's tummy.

A foal that is between one and two years old is called a yearling.

A horse is grown up at six. It is best not to ride it much until then.

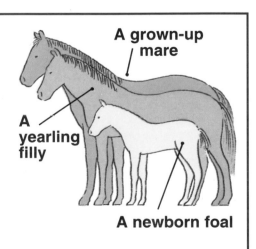

A grown-up mare

A yearling filly

A newborn foal

9

Horse colors

Horses and ponies come in lots of different colors. These have special names. Most horses are black, brown, bay or chestnut. Some horses have no color at all in their hair and skin. They are called albinos. They are pure white.

This black horse is a breed called Friesian. Friesians are always jet-black.

Color for camouflage

Some animals have colors that make them hard to see in the places where they live. This is called camouflage. When horses were wild, they grew coats with colors which helped them hide from danger.

Przewalski (say je-val-ski) horses come from the sandy parts of Mongolia. Their dun, or yellow-brown coats blend in with the ground there.

"Bay" means a rich red, golden, or brown body, with black legs, mane and tail.

There are different kinds of chestnut. Red chestnuts are a bright reddish color.

For horses, brown means this very dark brown shade.

This spotted horse is an Appaloosa. Some American Indians kept these horses because they liked their patterned coats. Appaloosas are often used in circuses.

The word "grey" is used for horses that are any shade of grey or white. A horse with dark grey rings on a pale grey coat, like this, is called dapple grey.

The two horses below are roans. They have dark coats with white hairs mixed in.

Blue roans have black coats with masses of white hairs.

Strawberry roans have chestnut coats with white hairs mixed in.

This beautiful golden color with a shining white mane and tail is called palomino.

Tall stories

Some people say chestnut horses get angry very easily. Spotted and part-colored horses are usually said to be well-behaved. Black ones are meant to be nasty or no good. In fact, a horse's color has nothing at all to do with what it is like, or how it behaves.

In fairy tales, grey horses are often kind and good.

Horses with patches of white and one other color are called part-colored. Black-and-white markings like this are called piebald, paint or Pinto.

Riding

People probably started to ride about 3,500 years ago. Riding changed their way of life. They could travel farther and faster than ever before. Today, we usually travel in cars, trains or planes; but people still ride for fun. Children find it easier to learn to ride on ponies, as they are smaller than horses.

The things ponies wear when they are being ridden are called tack.

The saddle helps the rider to sit comfortably. She puts her feet in the stirrups to balance better.

Ponies are friendly, so it is fun to take them out for rides together.

This pony is cantering. This is a fast, bounding movement.

Stirrup

The girth is a strap fastened around the pony's middle to hold the saddle in place.

This rider is wearing a hard hat. It helps to stop her from hurting her head if she falls off the pony.

The bridle helps the rider control the pony.

The bit is a piece of metal which goes in the pony's mouth.

The rider holds the reins. They are fastened to the bit.

When the rider twitches the reins, the pony feels the signals through the bit.

Breaking a pony in

Training a pony to be ridden is called breaking it in. This usually starts when the pony is about three years old.

It helps if the pony gets used to being touched as a foal.

The pony starts work on a long rein called a lunge. One person stands and holds the lunge. Another leads the pony in a circle.

The pony learns to carry some weight on its back. It wears a saddle for a few minutes, or a light person leans over it.

The pony is ridden on the lunge, with a bridle on. Once it obeys the rider, it can be ridden gently without wearing the lunge.

The pony learns more as it grows up and gets used to being ridden. It can do harder work like jumping when it is about five.

Looking after a pony

Caring for horses and ponies is quite complicated and can take a lot of time. People often start by keeping a pony, because most ponies are a bit tougher than horses. They can live out in a field nearly all year. This is one of the easiest ways to look after them.

At grass

This means the pony lives in a field, or paddock, most of the time. In winter, it may be put in a stable at night to keep warm.

The owner should visit the paddock twice a day to check that everything is all right.

A warm shelter with a roof keeps the pony safe from bad weather. The pony can also go there to get out of the sun.

A big paddock like this gives the pony lots of room to move about and get some exercise.

A pony gets bored and lonely if it is kept on its own. It is best to keep it with other ponies or a donkey for company.

The paddock should have plenty of short, juicy grass for the ponies to eat.

Keeping a pony in a stable

Another way of keeping a pony is in a stable. This keeps the pony safe, but it takes lots of work, too.

The stable has to be cleaned out twice a day. The pony also needs enough hay so it can eat day and night.

The pony must be taken out for at least two hours of exercise a day. This keeps it fit and happy.

Trees give the ponies some shade in hot weather.

There should be a trough full of fresh, clean water for the pony to drink.

A gate with a padlock is the safest way to get in and out. Ponies are clever and can work out how to pull bolts or lift latches.

A strong, high fence or hedge all the way around the paddock stops the ponies from getting out.

More about riding

Riding is exciting, but it is fairly difficult and takes a lot of practice to do well. Very good riders can teach their horses to do all sorts of tricky movements in a special type of riding called dressage (say dress-ah-je).

These horses are doing the hardest kind of dressage, called Haute Ecole (say oat eh-coll). This is French for "high school."

These horses are Lipizzaners. They are trained to do dressage movements at the Spanish Riding School, in Austria.

Riders at the Spanish Riding School wear this special uniform.

Movements like this help the horse to build up strong muscles. They also make its body move and stretch more easily.

This rider is not using stirrups. He balances by sitting deep down in the saddle.

This horse is doing a movement called a levade (say it luh-vaad.) It bends its back legs down low and balances on them. Then it lifts its front legs right up in the air.

The rider sits very still so that he does not make the horse lose its balance.

This horse is doing a movement called a capriole (say cap-ree-oll). It leaps off the ground with all four legs at once and kicks its back legs out behind.

The saddle has a roll of padding at the back and front to help the rider stay in place.

How a horse moves

Most horses have four ways of moving along, which are called gaits.

The walk is the slowest, steadiest gait. The horse moves smoothly, and lifts each foot one at a time.

The trot is a bouncy gait. The horse moves a front leg and a back leg from opposite sides, at the same time.

When it canters, the horse bounds. It puts a back foot down, then two opposite feet, then the last front foot.

The gallop is the quickest gait. The horse stretches out, and its feet hit the ground one at a time.

Horse travel

Before cars were invented, people used to travel in carts or carriages pulled by horses. Today, this kind of coach is still used in competitions and at horse shows. This is because coaches look lovely and driving them is exciting.

The reins are threaded through rings on the harness. This stops them from getting tangled in the coach wheels or in the horses' legs.

These little shields are called blinkers or winkers. They stop the horses from seeing things that might frighten them.

The horses wear a special driving harness. These collars help them to take the weight of the coach on their strong shoulders.

These horses are a breed called Gelderlanders. They are easy to train and very strong.

This sort of coach was used to carry passengers on long road journeys about 150 years ago.

A coach pulled by four horses, like this, is called a four-in-hand.

The driver is called the coachman. He controls the horses with long reins.

The long leather straps at the sides are called traces. One end is fastened to the coach. The other is clipped on to the horse's collar.

This is a road coach. It has four wheels, and there is room for people to sit on the top as well as inside.

Carts and caravans

This sort of carriage is called a chariot. The first ones were built about 5,000 years ago.

The troika is a Russian way of harnessing three horses in a row, across the front of a carriage.

Gypsy people travel from place to place. They sometimes live in caravans pulled by horses.

Working horses

Horses can do all sorts of work because they are strong and can move quickly. Today, people use machines for many jobs, but horses still do lots of different work all over the world.

This is an American cowboy. He is using his horse to help him catch this calf.

Horses for herding

In many places, horses are used to gather, or herd, animals. Here are some herding breeds.

Australian Stock Horse

This cowboy is riding in a way that is called Western riding. He sits right down in the saddle with his legs almost straight.

This is an American Quarter Horse. It can turn very fast to make the calf stop or go another way.

Criollo

Camargue

A good Quarter Horse like this one seems to know when to move, without being told.

Maremmana

Timor pony

Cowboys wear hats called Stetsons to keep the sun off their heads. They also wave them to make the cattle move on.

The cowboy holds the reins with one hand. He uses his free hand to make the calf move, or to catch it with his rope, called a lasso.

Young male cattle like this are called steers.

Other jobs

Police horses help to control crowds. They are very calm and well-behaved.

Pack ponies carry heavy luggage. They can pick their way over rocky ground where cars cannot go.

Some soldiers ride on horseback. This horse is carrying drums in an army parade.

In Britain, a few pit ponies still work in mines under the ground. They haul heavy things that the miners need.

Heavy horses

The biggest, strongest kinds of horses are called heavy horses. For hundreds of years, they did farm work in the fields. Now, machines do most of this work. But heavy horses are still sometimes used for jobs like pulling farm carts.

Percheron

This French breed is used all over the world for work such as dragging big loads.

Many heavy horses have long hair on their legs, but Percherons do not. This makes it easier for them to work on muddy ground.

The hooves are very hard and neat.

The Percheron has a massive, powerful body.

This breed is always either grey or black.

Its legs are thick and solid.

Heavy horses today

Heavy horses are sometimes used to pull brewers' drays. These are flat, long carts loaded with barrels of beer.

Metal ornaments called horse brasses may be put on the harness for decoration.

Heavy horses are often shown at horse shows with ribbons in their manes and tails.

Shire horse

Shire horses are the tallest and heaviest breed of all. They are usually between 16.2 and 18 hands high, but some grow even taller. A Shire can pull a load weighing five tonnes (tons). That is about five times its own weight.

Shire horses are huge and strong, but they are very gentle, too.

Shires can be black, brown, bay or grey. This is a bay.

Shires are still used quite a lot on farms in some countries.

Shires have masses of long, fine hair, called feather, around their feet. This is usually white.

This picture shows you how big a Shire horse is beside a pony and a man.

Show jumping

Show jumping is a sport where riders get their horses to jump lots of different fences. All horses can jump, but they need special training to become show jumpers. This can take several years.

The pricked-up ears show that the horse is happy and thinking hard about jumping the fence.

The rider leans over like this as the horse jumps. This helps it to carry him over the fence.

The rider looks over to where he wants the horse to land.

This horse is a German breed called a Hanoverian. It is very strong, with powerful muscles in its legs to help it jump really high.

The horse wears pads called brushing boots on its legs so they do not get bruised.

The rider leans up out of the saddle. She must balance carefully, to stay on.

To jump well, the horse needs to round its neck and back, as it springs into the air.

A good show jumper must be brave enough to try to get over big fences like this.

This horse is jumping a fence that is about 1.5 metres (5 feet) high. This is nearly as tall as the horse itself.

Show jumps

In a competition, the jumps are laid out in a special pattern called the course.

The horse has to obey the rider and jump the fences in the right order.

It often has to do sharp turns between all the different fences.

This is an upright fence. All the planks are placed above one another.

At a water jump, the horse must jump right over without landing in the water.

A wide jump with several poles placed side by side is called a spread.

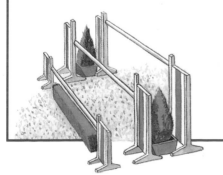

This wall is made out of wooden bricks so the horse does not get hurt if it knocks them down.

Gymkhanas and shows

A gymkhana is a competition where lots of riders and ponies get together to play games on horseback. These are called mounted games.

A mounted game

This is a bending race. The pony canters along and the rider steers it between the poles. They must weave in and out without knocking the poles over or missing any of the turns.

A game like this tests how nimble and quick the pony is. It must be able to twist and turn very fast and do as it is told.

The poles are set up in a long line, fairly close together.

Small ponies are often best at mounted games like this. They can turn more quickly than horses.

For a tricky game like this, the rider needs lots of practice.

A good gymkhana pony has to be very fit and full of energy.

The pony turns around the last pole and goes back the way it came.

More mounted games

In an obstacle race, the rider has lots of things to do on the way. This one is leading her pony and running along a row of flower pots.

In a flag race, the rider grabs one flag at a time and then gallops to put it in a flag holder down at the other end of the field.

In a sack race, the rider gallops to her sack. She jumps off the pony and into the sack. Then, leading her pony, she hops to the finish.

Showing a horse

At horse shows, there are often classes where a judge decides which is the most beautiful horse. Show horses need to be really well groomed. They should also be well-behaved.

A fine show horse has a well-shaped head and big, bright eyes.

This Welsh cob is being led around the ring. This is called showing a horse "in hand".

The horse's coat is brushed until it shines.

Eventing

In an eventing competition, the horse and rider do three different types of tests. These are dressage, show jumping, and cross-country riding.

Cross-country

In a cross-country test, the horse gallops across country and jumps huge fences as it goes. This shows how strong, brave, and fast it is, and how well it can jump.

The rider sits firmly in the saddle to keep his balance as the horse drops into the water.

At this jump, the horse has to land in the water. It will have to jump another fence to get out of the pool.

The horse drops down about one metre (three feet) into the water.

The water will come up to the horse's knees.

Cross-country fences are usually made out of things you see in the countryside, like tree trunks, gates and hedges.

Eventing horses have to be very strong and fit to get over a whole course of big, tricky jumps like this.

The dressage test

In the dressage test, the rider has to show how well-behaved the horse is. It has to do special movements in a space called an arena.

Show jumping

Dressage

The show jumping test

This is to show that the horse is nimble enough to jump over fences in a fairly small space. The jumps are smaller and closer together than the cross-country ones.

Unusual breeds

All horses and ponies are fairly alike in the way they look and behave. But some breeds have things about them that are a bit different.

Przewalski (say je-val-ski) horses

This breed is very rare and has never been tamed. There are none left in the wild, but some live in zoos. Scientists think that Przewalskis are very much like the first modern horses that ever existed.

Przewalski horses have pale rings around their eyes, and cream muzzles.

Akhal-Tekés have long, thin necks.

They look slim, but they are really strong.

Akhal-Teké horses

The Akhal-Teké (say ack-al-takey) is a very old breed from Russia. It can go for days without much food or water.

Akhal-Tekés often have shiny golden coats. This shade is very unusual in other horses.

This breed has long, spindly legs which make it very fast.

Scale

This picture shows you how big all of these horses and ponies look when they stand side by side.

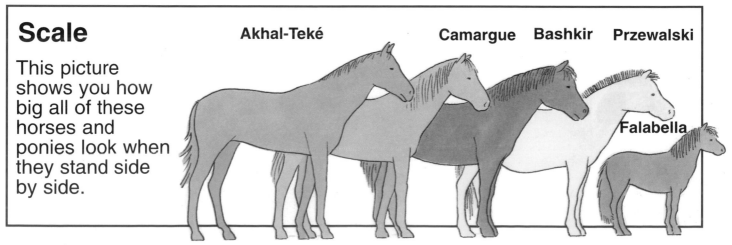

Akhal-Teké Camargue Bashkir Przewalski Falabella

Camargue horses

Herds of these horses roam free in a swampy part of France called the Camargue. Some of them are tamed and trained to help round up bulls.

These horses live on soggy, muddy land. They have to be very tough as they often get only spiky grass to eat and salty water to drink.

Grown-up Camargue horses are always grey.

Their foals are black, brown or dark grey. Their coats turn paler as they get older.

Bashkir ponies

Most horses and ponies have fine, smooth hair on their bodies, but the Bashkir pony has a curly coat. It is a strong breed which comes from Russia.

The hair in its mane and tail grows in long ringlets.

Falabella ponies

Falabellas come from Argentina. They are the smallest breed in the world. They grow to about 95 cm (30 inches) high, which is about the size of a big dog.

These ponies are gentle and good-natured.

In winter, the coat grows especially thick and curly. The curls can be up to 15 cm (6 inches) long.

These are grown-up Falabellas. You can see how tiny they are if you look at the scale picture on the opposite page.

This breed is too small to ride, so they are just kept as pets.

Index

The artwork on page 16 is based on an original photograph by Bob Langrish. The artwork on page 17 is based on a photograph used by kind permission of Michael Joseph Ltd.